Information Literacy and

FAKE NEWS

Diane Dakers

CRABTREE
PUBLISHING COMPANY
WWW.CRABTREEBOOKS.COM

CRABTREE
PUBLISHING COMPANY
WWW.CRABTREEBOOKS.COM

Author: Diane Dakers

Editors: Ellen Rodger and Janine Deschenes

Proofreader: Roseann Biederman

Design, photo research, and prepress:
 Tammy McGarr

Cover design: Ken Wright

Print coordinator: Katherine Berti

Photo Credits

Alamy: p 10 Ewing Gallowa; p 24 IanDagnall Computing;
 p 17 PJF Military Collection
iStock: p 6 (bottom left); p 9 (top); p 15 ©JayLazarin;
 p 26 ©GoodLifeStudio; p 35 (top right) ©bombuscreative;
 p 43 (top left) ©magnez2
NASA: p43 (top right)
Shutterstock: title page, p 22 ©Hadrian; p 5 ©Niloo;
 p 7 ©REDPIXELPL; p 18 ©1000 Words; p 19 ©ymphotos;
 p 23 ©AAraujo; p 25 ©testing; p 27 ©Anthony Correia;
 p 32 (bottom bkgd) ©Stefano Guidi; p 33 ©karen roach
Wikimedia: p 9 Stars and Stripes - US-Army; p 8 (inset);
 p 37; p 29 Leon Barritt

All other images from Shutterstock

Library and Archives Canada Cataloguing in Publication

Dakers, Diane, author
 Information literacy and fake news / Diane Dakers.

(Why does media literacy matter?)
Includes bibliographical references and index.
Issued in print and electronic formats.
ISBN 978-0-7787-4542-6 (hardcover).--
ISBN 978-0-7787-4546-4 (softcover).--
ISBN 978-1-4271-2038-0 (HTML)

 1. Fake news--Juvenile literature. 2. Information literacy--
Juvenile literature. 3. Journalism--Objectivity--Juvenile literature.
I. Title.

PN4784.F27D35 2018   j070.4'3   C2017-908096-2
                                                               C2017-908097-0

Library of Congress Cataloging-in-Publication Data

Names: Dakers, Diane author.
Title: Information literacy and fake news / Diane Dakers.
Description: New York : Crabtree Publishing, 2018. |
 Series: Why does media literacy matter? |
 Includes bibliographical references and index.
Identifiers: LCCN 2017060374 (print) | LCCN 2018005230
 (ebook) |
 ISBN 9781427120380 (Electronic) |
 ISBN 9780778745426 (hardcover) |
 ISBN 9780778745464 (pbk.)
Subjects: LCSH: Media literacy--Juvenile literature. | Fake news--
 Juvenile literature.
Classification: LCC P96.M4 (ebook) | LCC P96.M4 D35 2018
 (print) | DDC 302.23--dc23
LC record available at https://lccn.loc.gov/2017060374

Crabtree Publishing Company

www.crabtreebooks.com   1-800-387-7650

Printed in the U.S.A./052018/BG20180327

Published in Canada
Crabtree Publishing
616 Welland Ave.
St. Catharines, Ontario
L2M 5V6

Published in the United States
Crabtree Publishing
PMB 59051
350 Fifth Avenue, 59th Floor
New York, New York 10118

Published in the United Kingdom
Crabtree Publishing
Maritime House
Basin Road North, Hove
BN41 1WR

Published in Australia
Crabtree Publishing
3 Charles Street
Coburg North
VIC, 3058

Table of Contents

Media and Meaning

Every day, we are bombarded with pictures, videos, and words. Social media streams are full of news, opinions, and ads. Our smartphones are overrun with tweets, texts, and hashtags. This constant flood of information can be overwhelming. Some of it is valuable and informative. Some of it has been designed for dishonorable reasons— perhaps to shock us, make fun of someone, or **manipulate** ideas, thoughts, and **points of view**. With all this communication coming your way these days, it's hard to even know what's real.

The Meaning of Media

The exciting—and scary—part of the **digital world** in which we live today is that anyone with Wi-Fi and a smartphone can create content and send it around the globe within seconds. In the past, it wasn't that easy. Not just anyone could print a newspaper and have it delivered to thousands of households the same day. Today, anyone anywhere can publish a message, video, or photo, and someone somewhere—or millions of someones everywhere—will see it instantly.

LIVE BREAKING NEWS

Changing Communications

What has changed is the way we share information, or the media we use. Media is the plural form of the word medium. A medium is a method of **mass communication**, which is a way to deliver information to a wide variety of people. A newspaper is a medium that delivers printed stories. Radio delivers its messages by sound, and television broadcasts video images. The Internet uses digital technology which can be a mix of written, sound, and video messages.

The media are further divided into a few subcategories:

News media are organizations that specialize in delivering the news of the day. The TV news channel CNN, for example, is a news medium. So is the newspaper *The New York Times* or the magazine *Newsweek*.

Entertainment media include movies, TV shows, online games, magazines not related to news, and music videos.

Social media are such things as Facebook, Twitter, Snapchat, and Instagram.

All these media are ways to interpret and convey information and ideas. Some are a mixture of news and entertainment. Some also encourage interaction.

There are so many sources of information that it can be hard to know which ones to trust.

Media Literacy

The term "media literacy" has been around for decades. It means the ability to identify and understand different types of media and their messages.

Before the Internet was made available in the early 1990s, media literacy focused on print and broadcast media. Today, it includes digital media. This makes the subject much more complex. Media literacy requires developing skills that allow you to identify media messages, who produces them, and sometimes why they are produced. Simply put, being media literate means questioning everything you see, hear, and read online, on TV, on radio, in newspapers, and in magazines.

What is Truth?

Have you ever stopped to wonder who created your favorite video, and why that person made it? Is the video designed to entertain you, to sell you something, to persuade you to take action, or to stir up your emotions? Is the information in the video even real? These are important questions to consider when you interact with any type of information, no matter what its source. Unfortunately, in this era of "fake news," we can no longer accept everything we read, hear, or see as the truth. Can we really believe, for example, that sharks swam in the streets of Houston during Hurricane Harvey in September 2017? Or that Cheerios breakfast cereal contains paint thinner, as once reported? While it might seem obvious these stories fall into the fake news category, bogus information isn't always so easy to spot.

Media literacy skills can help you understand what news is and how to tell if it's true.

> "Even though the goal of journalism is to be impartial, almost every article is going to have some sort of a slant because every journalist is going to have a feeling and can't always necessarily hide that."
>
> ~ Robin Goldstein, journalism educator, Washington, DC

EXTRA! EXTRA
READ ALL ABOUT
DIRTY
LAUND
EXPOS

What's in a Name?

The term information literacy has been around longer than the term media literacy. And it has a slightly different meaning. Like media literacy, information literacy is about knowing how to find information you need, and how to recognize which material has value and which doesn't. It also involves knowing how to organize the information you find, and how to communicate it to others. Until the Internet became widely available in the 1990s, information literacy mostly related to libraries and research done in universities or colleges. The term media literacy includes many of the same things as information literacy. It applies the same concepts, such as determining what information is useful and trustworthy, but takes the ideas and **processes** out of the library and puts them to use for analyzing print, broadcast, and digital media.

DIG DEEP

For one day, keep track of all the different forms of media you engage with. Did you watch TV today? Write that down. Did you play a video game on your computer? Make note of that. Did you see an advertisement on the bus? Add that to the list. At the end of the day, look at your list—how long (or short) is it? How surprised (or not surprised) are you about the number of different ways people, organizations, and

CHAPTER 1

Making the News

Before we talk about "fake news," lets' talk about real news. News is information from a trusted source that impacts our lives. News can be positive or negative. When it comes to news, we have to take the good with the bad. News you don't like or don't agree with isn't fake news. It's just news you don't want to hear.

Who's Got News?

As long as people have inhabited the planet, they have shared information with each other. At one time, news was spread in person at a central meeting place in a village, by word-of-mouth, or by a messenger on horseback from a faraway town. About 1,300 years ago, officials in China began hand writing collections of news stories, and sharing them with the public. This practice spread around the world and continued until about 1440. That's when a German named Johannes Gutenberg invented a printing press with **moveable type**. This new device allowed the press operator to arrange metal letters into words, smear them with ink, and press them onto a piece of paper. That transferred the words to the paper. The inking process could be repeated over and over again to produce many copies of the same document.

The printing press made it easier to share the printed word with a large audience.

Books to Newspapers

Moveable type changed the world. Now, instead of one book being slowly written out by hand, hundreds of books could be printed in a shorter period of time. This led to more books being written and printed and more ideas being researched and explored. Soon, it became quick, easy, and less expensive to print a book, paper, or pamphlet. And that book, paper, or pamphlet could be distributed to hundreds of people at the same time.

More People Can Read

With reading material more available to "ordinary" people, more people learned how to read. When Gutenberg made his first press, only 30 percent of Europeans could read. Most people couldn't even spell their own names! "News" didn't exist and people believed rumor and myth. Over time, printing presses could print 250 pages an hour—much faster than a team of people writing by hand! By the mid-1800s, 62 percent of people in Europe and North America could read. Before long, people started using this new printing press to create newspapers. The era of mass communication was born. Today, roughly 80 percent of people in the United States can read, or are literate.

Newspapers spread news far and wide. Over the years, newspapers developed their own way of presenting information, using trusted sources for information. The news stories that had the most interest were put on the front page of the paper.

Newspapers Dominate

The spread of the printing press meant news could travel fast. Some of the world's first printed newspapers were published in the 1500s. The oldest paper still published today, was started in Haarlem, Netherlands in 1656. That's a long time to develop styles and methods for checking facts and printing information! Newspapers remained the public's main source of news until the 1920s when a new invention, the radio, began broadcasting newscasts. Twenty years later, television news took to the airwaves, and in the mid-1990s, the Internet made its debut. Today, we rely on all these media to deliver the news of the day. Each of them distributes news in a different way. But they all have a few things in common.

Most people didn't have televisions in their homes until the 1940s—if they could afford them. Families often watched programs together in the evenings. Television news wasn't common until the late 1940s.

24 NEWS

LIVE NEWS

DEVELOPING STORY

Manhunt continues for two suspects

Audience is Everything

One goal of all news media is to share relevant information with the public. News media are also businesses designed to make money for their owners. That means they are part public service and part **profit-making** activity. Media outlets stay in business by selling advertisements or subscriptions. Online, they sometimes get cash for clicks. This means that when you click on a link in a story, the site that sent you to that link makes a bit of money. The more people who watch, read, listen, or click, the more money the media makes. A second goal of every media outlet, then, is to reach as wide an audience as possible, to make sure they stay in business.

Method and Message

Each person **processes** information in a number of ways and different media appeals to different people. Newspapers appeal to people who want details and have the time to sit down and give a news story their full attention. TV news is faster paced, appealing to viewers who want the highlights of the day's news, but don't have time to read all about it. Television also offers a **multi-sensory** experience, with sounds, pictures, words, and storytellers. Some people prefer this style of news presentation.

Television news is visual and personality-driven. Watchers get to know and trust certain anchors, or presenters, and reporters.

Choose Your News

Not only do radio, TV, newspapers, and Internet draw different types of audiences, but audiences within each of those media are usually further divided. For example, some newspaper readers (both print and online) might prefer *The New York Times*, known for its high standards, in-depth coverage, and variety of news, feature stories, and columns. Other readers might find *The Times* dull or tiring to read. They might prefer the more upbeat *USA Today*, with its attention to color, images, design graphics, and stories on Hollywood actors. Similarly, some TV news viewers prefer CNN, while others choose FOX News. This is why there are so many media choices out there.

Radio and Internet

Radio often offers the quickest newscasts of all, delivering little more than the day's headlines. At the other extreme, though, are radio stations that do nothing but present news and information. These stations take time to analyze a story from a variety of **perspectives**. They discuss the day's events in detail with experts and knowledgeable journalists. People who like to listen to sounds, words, and storytellers while they do other things may prefer this type of radio news. The Internet is a blend of all media. It is a multi-media format that allows its audience to read through the news in a variety of ways. Internet also allows a person to sit quietly—anywhere, anytime—and read, watch, or listen to the news via a smartphone or tablet.

News Producers: Whose Angle?

Thousands of potential news stories happen every day, all around the world. Somebody has to decide which of those stories are worth sharing. That's the job of editors and producers. Editors are the people who choose the news for newspaper readers. Producers do the same for broadcast news viewers and listeners. Remember, though, the goal of a newspaper or newscast is to appeal to its audience. And each media outlet has a different audience. That means different news outlets often present different news stories on the same day. Even when they present the same stories, the angle, or how they present them will likely be different. That's because all news outlets have perspectives. A perspective is a viewpoint influenced by many factors. In news media, perspective includes the politics and world view of the media's owners, editors or producers, and writers. The media's owners will want to present stories that reflect their interests. They might also be influenced by advertisers and their perspectives. Editors and writers will have their own perspectives. Everyone has a perspective, but when perspective becomes a **bias** that prevents multiple points of views and voices from being heard, it steers away from being professional.

When examining news, it is important to know:

Who owns the news?

Who writes the stories?

Whose stories are told?

Who is missing from the stories?

How does this story reflect the interests of the news producer?

What Makes the News?

What makes news newsworthy is shaped by many factors. The people in charge of the media decide what stories get heard. In this way, they are **gatekeepers**, because they determine which, of the thousands of stories that could be told each day, are "newsworthy". Some things that editors and producers consider when deciding what is **newsworthy** are:

Location A story happening close to home is usually more important to local people than a faraway event.

Impact A story that affects many people is more newsworthy than one that matters to just a few members of the public.

Medium Some stories work better in certain media. For example, a TV producer might reject or downplay a particular story because there is no **compelling** video to go with it.

Within these general criteria, editors and producers also look for specific news "hooks" to grab an audience's attention.

Examples of news hooks include:

Something new—for example, a new law, a new techno-gizmo, or a new political leader

Something quirky, unusual, or shocking. An old newsroom adage, or saying, describes what is newsworthy this way: "If a dog bites a man, that is not news. When a man bites a dog, that is news." ~ **Attributed** to Charles Anderson Dana, American journalist, 1902

An update to a previous situation or event, such as a story about the aftermath of an earthquake.

A tragedy, crisis, or conflict situation such as a war, or as another old news media saying explains it: "If It Bleeds, It Leads."

Each day, editors and producers discuss possible news stories with reporters.

Reporters keep notes and often recordings, which they use to help them write their stories.

Reporting the News

A journalist, or reporter, is a person trained to find and present news stories for newspaper, radio, TV, and online audiences. Journalists learn to recognize a news story when they see it. They find out who they can trust to give them true information. They learn to report on all sides of a story.

Some journalists are assigned a beat, or a specific subject area to cover. For example, the health beat includes topics like medical discoveries such as a cure or treatment for a disease. The health beat also includes health care **policies** of a government

in office. Other beats include business, politics, police and crime, sports, and arts.

Over time, beat reporters become experts in their fields. They track ongoing stories and the characters involved in those stories. They come to understand the **lingo**, the laws, and the history of the beat. They develop sources, or people they trust to provide story ideas, tips, or insider information. Because of their knowledge of a subject area, beat reporters can add meaning, background, and insight to a story that other reporters can't.

Anatomy of a News Story: the 5Ws

When a reporter writes a news story, he or she answers five basic questions—who, what, when, where, and why. Who is involved in the story? What happened? When did it happen? Where did it happen? Why did it happen? These five questions are called the 5Ws. Sometimes, the journalist also adds an H—for how. Other times, the answers to the 5Ws take care of the H.

The Inverted Pyramid

The structure of a news story is called the "inverted pyramid." That means the most important information comes first, followed by less-crucial details. The least important material comes toward the end. The first sentence of a story, called the "lede"—yes, that is how it's spelled—is designed to grab the reader's attention and summarize the article. For example, a crime story might begin with, "A robber made off with $5 million worth of diamonds in a jewelry store heist yesterday." Instantly, the reader knows what the story is about. The 5Ws come next in the article, giving the person reading or listening the need-to-know facts up front. That way, if the person has to walk away for some reason, he or she still gets the essential information.

Important information

Less crucial details

Least important details

How do we know the news from a warfront is true? When news media is at or near the action, they get the story as it happens. Or they can interview people who witness the event firsthand.

Journalism as a Profession

Unfortunately, because news media are businesses that need to make money, and because it's costly to have a journalist dedicated to a single subject area, beat reporters are vanishing at many media outlets. Today's reporters often have to be **generalists** and write about a variety of subjects. Similarly, investigative journalism is gradually disappearing from the news media. Investigative journalism is the practice of researching, interviewing, and digging deeply into a single story, usually to expose wrongdoing. It can take weeks, months, or even years to conduct such a thorough investigation. But time is money the business side of the media often can't afford to spend. To cut costs, today's news media rely more and more on freelance reporters. These are trained journalists who are paid per story, rather than a staff reporter who has the security of a regular paycheck. Some media are also putting their trust in members of the general public, or **citizen journalists**.

Citizen Journalists Give Immediate Coverage

Citizen journalists are ordinary people, as opposed to trained journalists, who post commentary, photographs, and videos of news and events online. They are bloggers, Instagrammers, YouTube Channel hosts, and other people who often happen to be in the right place at the right time—with a cell phone and a social media account. Think about the **Arab Spring** uprisings in 2010 and 2011, when people in many countries in the Middle East protested, rioted, and rebelled against their governments. Often, journalists from foreign news outlets couldn't get to these hotspots. Some couldn't get there fast enough or didn't stay long enough. Protesters with camera phones supplied thousands of photos and videos for media outlets around the world.

We are now used to seeing immediate coverage of events such as earthquakes or war posted by citizen journalists. The media has reacted to these news reporters in a number of ways. Some media has encouraged it. Using citizen journalist material is often cheaper than sending their own journalists. They also allow for immediate first-hand accounts of news and more **diverse** coverage. This is particularly true in areas of the world unfamiliar to foreign media. Citizen journalists may know the issues and geography better and may be more able to explain things. But just as professional journalists must ensure the information they are getting is correct, media outlets must ensure the news they are getting from citizen journalists is accurate and **verified**.

DIG DEEP

Today, most people carry phones with built-in cameras and video recorders. Many citizen journalists blog about news and events, or create social media venues where everyone can anonymously post photos, videos, and comments. Because the public's eyes and ears are now on the job, do you think we still need "real," or trained, journalists? Why or why not?

"We Are All Khaled Said"

The Arab Spring uprisings in 2010 were pro-**democracy** protests. Many of the protesters who took photos and videos were killed or otherwise punished for daring to show the world what was happening in the many Middle Eastern countries at the time. Because of this, many people posted images using false names and social media accounts.

A young boy takes part in an Arab Spring protest in Yemen. Uprisings took place in many Middle Eastern countries from 2010-2012.

One of those was an Egyptian named Wael Ghonim. In June 2010, he anonymously launched a Facebook page titled "We Are All Khaled Said." Wael named the site after a young man who was beaten to death by police in Egypt. Within eight months, the site had become "the biggest **dissident** Facebook page in Egypt," according to *The New York Times*. Angry Egyptians used the site as a place to post anonymous photos and videos and to plan protests. This site was used to organize the protests in 2011 that eventually toppled the Egyptian government. Days after they began, police discovered that Wael was the anonymous administrator of the Facebook page. They arrested him and threw him in jail where he was blindfolded and tortured. Because the international press picked up Wael's story, the Egyptian government gave in to global pressure and freed him after 11 days. Wael was nominated for the 2011 Nobel Peace Prize for for his innovative use of social media in inspiring the protests.

Sources and Reliability

One thing trained journalists do on the job is build relationships with trusted sources. Trusted sources are usually people in-the-know about a particular subject, such as experts who are in a position to hear news before it's made public. Trustworthy sources must have nothing to gain, personally or financially, from sharing a news story. To earn a journalist's trust, they also have to be reliable, meaning they can be trusted to supply real information—no fake news allowed. Experienced journalists eventually develop an instinct for knowing who's telling the truth and who's inventing things. Still, to be sure every story is true and accurate, a good reporter confirms new information by double-checking with a variety of resources.

CHAPTER 2

Different Views = Different News

Bias is something we all have. It isn't necessarily good or bad. It just means we have opinions and preferences. We form biases because of our backgrounds, our experiences, and our personal points of view. Bias is one of those things that makes us individuals. When it comes to news stories, though, a journalist's bias shouldn't show.

Point of Truth or Point of View?

Because we are bombarded with so much information every day, it can be hard to know what is true (the facts) and what is someone's belief (an opinion). Here are some guidelines to help you recognize the differences between the two:

Opinion

Cannot be proven true or false

Can be changed

Based on feelings, thoughts, experiences

Examples: Apples are delicious.
Lego is the best toy ever.
Alligators are scary.

Fact

Can be proven to be true or false

Cannot be changed

Based on research, evidence, statistics

Examples: Apples grow on trees.
Lego was invented in Denmark.
Alligators need food to survive.

Does Bias Mean It's Not Accurate?

Journalists are trained to present all sides of a news story. We expect them to be unbiased in their reporting. We watch and listen to news and read newspapers and sites to find out what's going on in the world and not to hear reporters' opinions about what's going on in the world. We trust journalists, and the news media they represent, to verify facts, to offer a variety of **perspectives** on a given subject, and to update us on issues that impact our lives. These accurate details, observations, and background materials allow us to form personal opinions on the topic in question. But journalists are human, and even though they're trained to keep their opinions out of the news, bias can sneak in through things such as **tone**, and the style and depth of coverage. It can even leak in through the bias of the sources a journalist uses. Likewise, news outlets can exhibit the biases of their owners or senior managers, even when those biases are not **explicit**.

> "Even though the goal of journalism is to be impartial, almost every article is going to have some sort of a slant because every journalist is going to have a feeling and can't always necessarily hide that."
>
> ~ Robin Goldstein, journalism educator, Washington, DC

Media should offer a number of perspectives when reporting on issues.

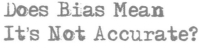

CLOSER LOOK

Who Wants Unbiased News?

People often grumble that the news is politically biased, especially when they hear or read something they don't like. But is this the opinion of most **consumers** of news? According to a 2018 report by the Pew Research Center, people around the world overwhelmingly agree that news should be unbiased. Their beliefs on whether it is biased depends a lot on where they live and who they would vote for.

Pew Research Center is an American **think tank** that asks people their opinions and puts the results together in reports. In the United States, Pew found that only 56 percent of people polled thought political news was reported accurately and only 47 percent thought political issues were reported fairly. In Canada, 78 percent believed their news media reported accurately and 73 percent thought political issues were reported fairly.

Seventy-five percent of Germans felt that their news was reported accurately and 72 percent said they thought political issues were reported fairly. By contrast, in France, only 62 percent thought news was accurately reported and 47 percent believed political issues were reported accurately. Those countries with the least amount of faith in unbiased political reporting

included Argentina, Chile, Colombia, South Korea, Greece, and Spain. The report said political identification, or who the people who were polled would vote for, influenced people's beliefs about whether they thought the news was biased or unbiased. "The U.S. is one of only a few countries where governing party supporters are less satisfied with their news media than are nonsupporters," the report said.

Politics is everywhere, especially in news. People everywhere like their media to be unbiased. What people consider to be biased news has a lot to do with the politics they support.

Ownership and Point of View

Let's say the owner of a media company likes a particular politician or political point of view. It's possible that a TV station owned by that person may present news in a way that supports that particular politician or point of view. This can become an even bigger problem when a single owner runs many different media companies. In Canada, for example, one particular corporation owns TV and radio stations across the nation, along with specialty channels, magazines, and websites. The company also provides cable TV, satellite, Internet, and cell phone services across the country. That means one company controls much of the content Canadians watch, read, and listen to. It also controls the ways they receive that content.

Some countries have laws and rules in place to make sure a single organization, or a small number of organizations, can't control all (or most of) the news and information media in that country. Other nations have no such regulations. Taking into account the discussion about bias, do you think such laws are beneficial or harmful to members of the public? Explain your opinion.

The Role of Advertising

The fight for advertising dollars further complicates the news business. In the past, the public service (news) and business (advertising) sides of a media outlet were supposedly separate. They had no influence on each other. Today, as media companies struggle to survive financially, the line between the two is blurry. It's not uncommon for a television station to run an upbeat news story about a company owned by a major advertiser. The flip side of that is that a news department may be forbidden from running a news story that could offend local advertisers, for fear of losing business. This can lead to bias in the news. Some news outlets make no secret of their political, social, and business attitudes. Sometimes, though, the biases are hard to spot. It's important, then, to research news media to find out which ones you can trust to present balanced news reports and tell the whole story.

Advertising plays a key role in keeping media afloat. Without the money advertisers pay to place their ads (such as on the front page of this newspaper), most media would close. That means media outlets walk a fine line between keeping readers and pleasing advertisers.

Clues in the News

Figuring out whether a news story is biased takes a bit of detective work. Here are some clues to help you uncover bias in the news:

Consider the language in a news story. For example, does the reporter use words like "claimed," "demanded," or "argued"? These words suggest the person who spoke them is expressing an opinion, rather than a fact. This may be a clue to possible reporter bias as it is intended to shape your opinion of the source. How would your opinion differ if the reporter instead used the word "said"?

Who is interviewed or quoted first in the story? Which side of the story gets more focus? Often, the voice that gets the most attention is the side the journalist agrees with, or is biased toward.

Where in the newspaper, TV newscast, or website does the story appear? The higher up in the news presentation a story is, the more likely readers or viewers will pay attention to it. That means the story is important—in the opinion of editors or producers.

Does the story include a variety of points of view? If everyone quoted in the story is saying the same thing in different ways, that suggests bias.

Does the media outlet have a known, or obvious, bias toward a particular point of view? If so, stories may be slanted toward that perspective.

Look at photographs and videos that accompany a news story. Is a particular person shown looking angry, sloppy, or creepy, while another person is represented with a smiling, well-dressed, trustworthy image? Photographs often indicate bias toward or against a particular person or subject.

Images can display points of view and biases as well, and sometimes better, than words.

DIG DEEP

Read a story from an online news site. Using the criteria for determining bias, analyze the story. Is it balanced or biased? Can you guess the reporter's opinion on the subject from reading the story? Is one side of the issue better presented than the other? Do you see bias when you "read between the lines"?

> " The purpose of journalism is to provide citizens with the information they need to make the best possible decisions about their lives, their communities, their societies, and their governments.
>
> ~ The American Press Institute, 2017 "

Looking For Lies

Detecting bias in news stories is an important skill to have in your media literacy toolbox. Sadly, though, it's no longer enough. On top of determining bias in our news reports, we now have to watch for outright lies. Technology such as Wi-Fi and cell phones make it easy for people with social media accounts to post anything online. It doesn't matter if what they post is true or not. Like citizen journalism, this new media reality comes with pros and cons. The upside is that everyone in the world—including you—has a platform to voice thoughts and ideas. The downside is that not all of those voices tell the truth. Just as quickly as you can post a photo on your social media site, a dishonorable person can post a "fake news" story. That makes it hard to know what to believe anymore.

Alternative or Distortion?

When people think the **mainstream** media sources of news are too biased, they might look elswhere for news. It's good to get a different perspective, and there are many legitimate sources of news beyond the mainstream. But if the news you find on the Internet seems to present stories that are hard to believe, it likely means your lie detecting skills are working. That's a good thing. Many "alternative" news sites are little more than opinion blogs. It's important to know that the truth you are presented with might not be true, or could be slanted by bias. But there is no such thing as "alternative facts". When you are finding misinformation presented about things you know to be true, don't fall for it. Use the guidelines for determining bias. Be wary of **slants** that reflect only one point of view. Don't spread news that is **unsubstantiated**. And steer clear of **conspiracy theories**. These are ideas that say certain events occur because of secret plots by powerful people or groups. People who believe in conspiracy theories don't believe facts. They spread fear based on their worldviews.

Soon after the 9/11 terrorist attacks on New York in 2001, some people began to spread conspiracy theories about them.

CHAPTER 3

Fake News and Lies

You've probably heard a lot of talk about "fake news" in the media. Fake news is false information that is deliberately passed off as true—and it's nothing new. Fake news has been around as long as people have shared information with each other.

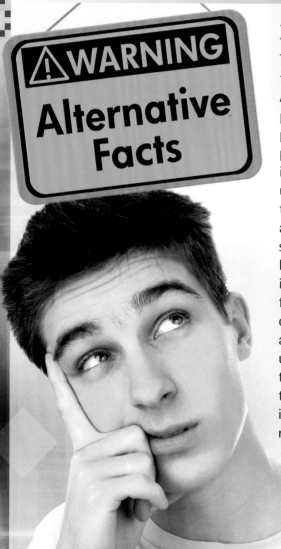

⚠ WARNING
Alternative Facts

Lies By Other Names

The term fake news has been out there for more than a century. First used in American newspapers in the 1890s, the phrase didn't catch on widely. Instead, people used other words such as lies, propaganda, and false news to describe intentional **misinformation**. It wasn't until late 2016 that fake news took the spotlight. In the past, other words and phrases were used to describe the spread of false news and information. Propaganda is false or exaggerated information used to help gain support for a particular cause, to sway public opinion, or otherwise influence citizens' attitudes. During wartime, governments use propaganda to boost approval for their troops and to reinforce a dislike of the enemy. They also use it to encourage individuals to help the fight by joining the military or supporting the war financially.

"Yellow journalism" is another historical term for fake news. Yellow journalism is news reporting that uses over-the-top language, one-sided storytelling, made-up interviews, and false facts to attract an audience. The term was first used in the 1890s when a pair of New York newspapers fought a heated battle for readers and advertisers. They tried to outdo each other with **scandalous**—and often phony—stories. At the time, one of the papers carried a popular color comic strip with a character called the Yellow Kid. When the second newspaper lured the comic strip artist away, the first paper hired a new artist to draw a new Yellow Kid. To attract readers, each paper gave more and more space to its version of the beloved character. This "battle of the yellow kids" led to the phrase "yellow kid journalism," which was soon shortened to "yellow journalism."

This Yellow Kid themed cartoon illustrates the competition between newspapers owned by Joseph Pulitzer and William Randolph Hearst during the **Spanish American War** (1898). The papers fought to outdo each other in outrageous stories and whipping up the public's anger with fake news about the Spanish.

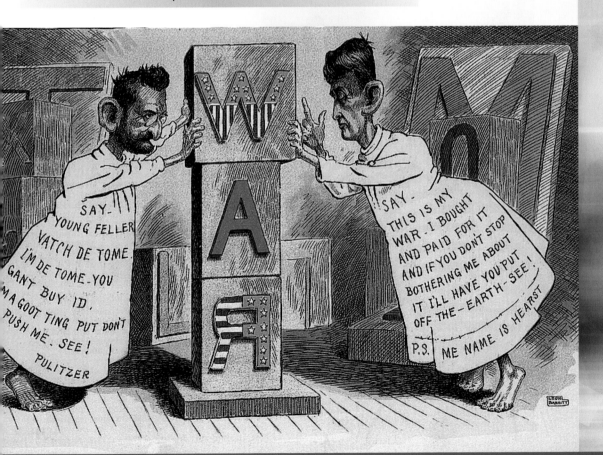

Aliens Have Landed and Other Sensational News

Sensationalism is similar to yellow journalism, except it often contains nuggets of truth. Like yellow journalism, sensationalism uses misleading language, shocking headlines, and ridiculous photographs to grab audience attention. "Aliens Land in Backyard!" might be the front-page headline on a supermarket tabloid, for example. When you buy the newspaper and read it, though, you may find just a silly story about someone who saw a weird light behind his or her house and joked, "I think an alien just landed in our backyard." The goal of sensationalism, like yellow journalism, is to encourage people to click on web links, buy newspapers, or watch videos.

Whatever it's called, fake news is disguised as genuine news. Its goal is to trick audiences into believing it is real. When readers and viewers share the bogus information with others, the lie spreads. In the past, news traveled by word of mouth, or through newspapers, television, and radio. Today, because of social media and the Internet, news—and fake news—spreads at lightning speed. And thanks to technology, fake news looks more real than ever. That makes it tough to spot.

Fake News Checklist

Figuring out whether a news story is fact or fiction takes a bit of detective work. Here are some clues to help you uncover fake news:

☑ Beware ALL CAPS, exclamation marks!!! and words such as "amazing," "shocking," or "you'll never believe ..." Headlines containing these elements are often click bait, designed to grab your attention, lead you to a new website, and to spread a story fast and far.

☑ Is the website hosting the story **credible**, or is it known for carrying fake news? Click on the "about" section for hints to its reliability. Double-check the information on sites you trust, or visit a fact-checking site such as snopes.com.

☑ Look at the website's url. Phony newsmakers are sneaky. Sometimes, they insert the name or logo of a legitimate news site on a fake news article to make it look real. If, for example, a story appears to be from NBC news, but the url doesn't say NBC in it, chances are it's fake. Compare the url, (in this case, to the real NBC news) to be sure.

☑ Look for typos, spelling mistakes, and bad grammar. **Legitimate** sources have proofreaders.

☑ If nobody is quoted in an article, be suspicious. Also be suspicious of "anonymous" sources.

☑ Consider photos and videos. Do they look impossible? For example, a video of an eagle carrying away a 50-pound child is probably fake. Also, think about the photographer—is it even possible that someone could have taken that photo or video?

☑ Do you feel anger, shock, or disgust when you read the story or watch the video? Real news stories are designed to provide information, not to evoke an emotional response.

> "The speed of communications is wondrous to behold. It is also true that speed can multiply the distribution of information that we know to be untrue."
>
> ~ Edward R. Murrow, American journalist, 1964

31

What's the Point?

You might wonder why anyone would go to the trouble of creating fake news. After all, isn't there enough real information out there already? The short answer is that creating fake news is easy. Remember, anyone with Internet and a computer, tablet, or smart phone can create and deliver instant information to the world. For some people, sending out bogus news stories may simply be a thrill, or a challenge to see how many readers they can trick. More often, though, fake news is spread by **dishonorable** people who have something to gain by lying to the public. They might do it to further a cause. Making or spreading a fake news story about a public figure or politician can draw people to read the story and believe it. Readers might be swayed to dislike that person, not see them as **reputable**, or as someone who should not be in public office. Some people make fake news for money. Think about headlines you see on gossip magazines at the grocery store checkout: UFO Crashes on the Outskirts of Town! The Secret Tearing These (Celebrity) Sisters Apart! Such grabby banners are designed to convince customers to pay money to buy the magazine, and read on. Many of the stories are just plain lies. Others are dramatic or twisted versions of the truth. Similarly, when you click on a catchy headline or photo on a website, a new site opens. The original site makes a bit of money for sending you to the new one.

News +++ Information +++ News +++ Information +++ News +++ Information +++ News

Aliens Have Landed!

Goodbye Best-Selling Treat? Or Cruel Hoax?

A September 2017 "news" story posted on Facebook reported that Reese's Peanut Butter Cups were about to be taken off the market. Within days, tens of thousands of people had clicked on the story—and shared it with hundreds of thousands of their friends. Chocoholics panicked and called the company to find out if the rumor was true! Not only was the story not true, but the sweet treat continues to be the number-one selling candy bar on the market in the United States. It turns out the story had been completely made up and posted on www.breakingnews365.net, a site that invites users to "prank your friends now."

World's most popular candy to be removed from shelves by October 2017

Thursday 14 September 67960 Shares

Share on Facebook

FAKE NEWS

The Reese's story fooled a lot of people. Why would the world's most popular candy be discontinued? If a story sounds like a fib, chances are it is. It's best to check before spreading it.

FACT OR FICTION?

REESE'S PEANUT BUTTER CUPS BEING DISCONTINUED?

The Damage Done

Sometimes, people cook up fake news to make themselves look better in the eyes of the world, or to gain sympathy. Like wartime **propaganda**, fake news stories are often used today to turn members of society against a particular group of people. This creates a common enemy, a target for anger and dissatisfaction—someone to blame for social problems instead of criticizing government **policies**. Today, most fake news is designed to influence public opinion—to convince people to agree (or disagree) with a certain point of view, to support (or oppose) a cause, or even to win an election at all costs.

During World War II, government War Bonds posters were a form of propaganda used to raise money to fund the war. They used patriotic images to make people feel guilty.

BUY WAR BONDS

Lies or Leanings?

Bias in the news and fake news are equally difficult to detect, but they're not quite the same thing. Here are some guidelines to help you recognize the differences between the two:

Fake News

Disguised as real news stories

False information

Intentional deception

Often difficult to detect

Bias

Embedded in real news stories

Favoritism toward one side of a story

Often unintentional

Often difficult to detect

Who Creates Fake News?

In 2016, a bunch of teenagers in southeast Europe struck fake news gold. They launched websites with the sole purpose of making money by peddling outrageous news, mostly about American politics and other **"trending"** topics. Articles in *The Guardian* newspaper and *Wired* magazine revealed that there were over 100 fake news sites operating out of the town of Veles, Macedonia. The sites were started by teens and other young people looking for a way to make easy money. They set up the sites, swiped or **plagiarized** content from blogs and websites published in the United States, and posted the links on Facebook. The fake news earned the Macedonian teens pennies per click through automated advertising engines that measured how many people came to the sites. The clicks added up. Millions of people—most of them in the United States—read the posts. Some fake news sites earned thousands of dollars within four to six months. The fake news frenzy forced Facebook and Google to change the rules on advertising and misleading news sites. Still, many sites changed tack and started focusing on other fake news topics.

DIG DEEP

Write a fake news story. How many people can you fool? (Be honest with your readers after you fool them. Make sure they know it's fake news!) Do you think most members of the public are aware of how easy it is to be tricked by fake news and information? Does it matter? Why or why not?

CHAPTER 4

Truth and Consequences

Everybody has the right to an opinion, but opinions are not facts. Questioning information is good, but ignoring or rejecting evidence because it suits already formed beliefs is not critical thinking.

> Everybody, you and I, we have a role to play [in stopping the spread of fake news]. We are the ones who share the content. We are the ones who share the stories online. In this day and age, we are all publishers and we have responsibilities.
>
> ~ Journalist Stephanie Busari, TED Talk, 2017

How Fake News Does Real Harm

One of the things that distinguishes fake news from real news is how fake news is intended to inspire outrage within the reader. That outrage can urge the reader to action. Sometimes the action is simple, such as sharing or spreading the article to friends without checking if it is true. A fake news article might even ask readers to "share if you agree." Fake news can have an influence on readers' attitudes and behavior. Occasionally, it can even be dangerous.

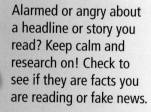

Alarmed or angry about a headline or story you read? Keep calm and research on! Check to see if they are facts you are reading or fake news.

Pizzagate: When Fake News is Dangerous

In the fall of 2016, a series of fake news stories almost led to disaster. The stories, about a pizzeria in Washington, D.C., being a front for a **child trafficking** ring, were shared on social media sites such as Twitter and Reddit. The fake news stories had their root in an online message board **conspiracy theory** that United States presidential candidate Hillary Clinton and a top aid were running the ring with the pizzeria. The stories spread quickly on social media. Soon, the pizzeria owner was getting death threats, and his staff was **harassed**. Protesters set up shop near the restaurant and questioned the owner on video. The video was put up on YouTube to try to prove he was a criminal mastermind. A few months later, a gunman took it upon himself to "investigate" the situation. He stormed into the pizzeria and started shooting. When he discovered there were no children locked away in the restaurant— or anywhere else—he gave himself up to police. Fortunately, nobody was hurt in the incident. The gunman was later sentenced to 48 months in jail for his crime. Still, the power of fake news is so strong that despite being declared untrue, some people still believe the story was real.

The Pizzagate rumor began on a message board, but was spread on Twitter and Facebook. Nobody spreading the story bothered to check whether it was true.

The Fallout of Fake News and Untruths

This fake news story—now known as "Pizzagate"—is an extreme example of the harm that lies, rumors, and access to social media can do. All it takes is someone to make up a story and post it online. Almost anyone with some skill and the right computer software can doctor photos or videos. With knowledge of Photoshop for example, you can take a picture of a protest and insert the image of a person who wasn't there.

What is True?

It's fairly simple to write and post a false social media story that says a swim coach abuses animals. It's also possible to doctor a recording of someone's voice to string words together in a way that person never used them. Some fake news looks or sounds so legit that many people can't tell the difference and are fooled. One **consequence** of fake news is that many people don't know what to believe anymore. What is true? What is made up? Figuring this out, using media literacy skills, takes work—time and effort that some people can't spare. Or they don't care enough to bother, so they stop paying attention altogether. They stop participating, discussing, and forming opinions about the news of the world. This can cause problems when it comes to issues that affect our lives such as politics, elections, and science, for example. Citizens who have turned a blind eye to the issues may not care enough, or may be too confused, to vote. That means fewer people make important decisions about who leads our cities, states, and nations.

yeah right!

Being skeptical can be a good trait when it comes to analyzing the news.

Distrust of the Media

Another consequence of the recent flood of fake news is a distrust of news media in general. Some people are so fed up with the bogus stories that they assume that every news story is a lie. Then there are individuals who insist the news media are plotting against them by reporting false facts. United States President Donald Trump, for example, says all news media (except one) are "fake media" trying to make him look bad.

In recent years, fake news stories that accuse people of racism, terrorism, spying, sexual assault, and other wrongdoing have caused harm to people's lives, careers, and businesses. In spring 2017, in a small town just outside London, England, someone (still unidentified) posted a fake photo on Snapchat. The picture showed a local take-out restaurant infested with cockroaches. The message with the photo said the restaurant served a side of cockroach with a chicken dinner shared by a group of students. The photo spread quickly on social media, and business at the popular student hangout tanked. Within a month, sales were so bad that the owner put the restaurant up for sale. The photo and message were quickly proven false, but the damage was done. The restaurant was guilty in the eyes of the community.

Would you believe a story shared on Snapchat about a restaurant serving cockroaches with its dinners?

DIG DEEP

Of course you don't believe Earth is flat. But you have beliefs of your own. Look at your social media newsfeeds. Are a variety of points of view represented? Or do all your contacts think the way you do? Pick one issue that you and your friends agree upon. Do some research to find another opinion on that issue. Consider and discuss the other side of the story with your friends. Does the new information change your opinion? What can you learn from people who disagree with you?

Can you have conversations with your friends where you share different opinions on an issue?

Confirmation Bias

One reason people might believe fake news is because such stories confirm beliefs they already hold. For example, there are people out there in the world who believe the Earth is flat. To them, any story about a pancake-shaped planet is true. They might belong to social media sites where they share news about a flat Earth. They would dismiss round-Earth reports and photos as fake. This is called "confirmation bias." It means we value information that agrees with our beliefs and ignore information that disagrees. The result, in this case, is that the flat-Earth people stop questioning the shape of the planet because they know it's flat, and they have the evidence (the fake news stories) to prove it.

Clues in the News

Figuring out which websites you can trust to provide true and accurate information takes a bit of detective work. Here are some clues to help:

☑ If a website is associated with a respected newspaper, television network, or radio station, it is likely trustworthy. Similarly, websites connected to universities, colleges, and libraries are also typically trustworthy. Just make sure the site actually is connected to the media outlet or college in question—see clue #2.

☑ Check the url. Websites that end in .com, .org, .gov, .net are usually safe. In Canada, .ca, and in Britain, .uk, are also likely to be legit. However, if other letters are tacked on to the end of these common urls, be suspicious.

☑ Read the "About" section of a website to find out where it's based and who is associated with it. If there is no "About" section, or no contact information, beware.

☑ Sites with obvious errors can't be trusted. Be wary of errors that are not corrected.

☑ Don't trust a site that doesn't identify who posted a particular story or video and when. Credible websites list content creators and date.

☑ Sites that bombard you with ads, especially pop-up ads, are also suspicious. Providing credible information is usually not the goal of such sites—typically, they're out to sell you something.

Over time, being a fact sleuth will become second nature.

Rules that Rule: Codes of Ethics

Most legitimate, or genuine, news outlets follow codes of **ethics**. These are documents that outline acceptable and unacceptable behavior for everyone who works at an organization. Media and journalism societies often have similar rules about the personal behavior of reporters, editors, producers, and photographers. These rules of conduct include being fair, telling the truth, and being accurate. These rules ensure that a media outlet or organization remains trustworthy in the eyes of its readers, listeners, and viewers.

To maintain that trust, stories in legitimate news outlets usually go through a series of checks and balances before they reach their audiences. For example, a number of different editors will review a single story before it becomes public. Some check for bias, legal, and content concerns. Others look out for typos, and grammar and spelling errors. Many media outlets also have fact-checkers, who do nothing but confirm that a story's details are correct. In print media, proofreaders give the story one final once-over before it is published.

That's not to say mainstream media outlets never make mistakes. If something slips through, and a reader or viewer points it out, codes of ethics require that legitimate news organizations publish, post, or air a correction.

Despite overwhelming evidence, some people still don't believe humans ever landed on the moon.

The Opposite of Fake News

You've probably heard the saying, "Truth is stranger than fiction." Maybe because of that, some people choose to believe the fiction instead of the facts. They believe some real stories are actually fake.

The most famous example of this is the 1969 moon landing. On July 20 of that year, American astronauts Neil Armstrong and Edwin "Buzz" Aldrin became the first humans to set foot on the moon. The two men planted a flag on the lunar surface, snapped a few pictures, took a walk, and collected some scientific samples. Today, more than 50 years later, despite scientific proof, some people still say the moon landing never happened. They say it was staged at a film studio on Earth.

Another example of real news that some believe is fake is The **Holocaust**. During **World War II**, six million Jews in Europe were forced from their homes, sent to prison camps, and killed by the **Nazi regime**. Some people say this never happened. Others say Jews were deported, not killed. Still others believe only a few thousand Jews were murdered. Sadly, there is overwhelming evidence—including eye witnesses, documentation, and photographs—to prove otherwise.

> "If you can convince people that real news is fake, it becomes much easier to convince them that your fake news is real."
>
> ~ Garry Kasparov, Chair of Human Rights Foundation

43

Bibliography

Introduction

"Media Literacy Defined." National Association for Media Literacy Education. https://namle.net/publications/media-literacy-definitions/

Chapter 1

"What is the Purpose of Journalism?" American Press Institute. http://bit.ly/TIF1my

Dana, Charles Anderson. Quote Investigator http://bit.ly/2tnPlXZ

Vargas, Jose, Antonio. "Spring Awakening: How an Egyptian Revolution Began on Facebook." *The New York Times*, Feb 17, 2012. http://nyti.ms/2FlCbvX

Goldstein, Robin. "Fake News Vs. Media Bias." FHS View blog (Flint High School), 2017. http://bit.ly/2oWOOXx

Chapter 2

"Publics Globally Want Unbiased News Coverage but are Divided on Whether Their News Media Deliver." Pew Research Center, 2018. http://pewrsr.ch/2EyoDg7

Baluja, Tamara. "Diversity of Media Ownership Literally Non Existent in Canada." J-Source, Canadian Journalism Project, 2015. http://bit.ly/2zL8ZPG

"How To Detect Bias in News Media." Fair.org http://bit.ly/2IaTrGj

"What is the Purpose of Journalism?" American Press Institute website. http://bit.ly/1R1zz3A

Murrow, Edward R. Family of Man Award speech. Protestant Council of the City of New York,1964.

Chapter 3

"Ten Questions for Fake News Detection." The News Literacy Project. http://bit.ly/2hWjpC2

Machcinski, Anthony, J. "No, Your Reese's Peanut Butter Cups Aren't Going Anywhere, Company Says." York Daily Record, Sept. 27, 2017. http://bit.ly/2Hfz9tK

Subramanian, Samanth. "Inside the Macedonian Fake-News Complex." *Wired* magazine, 2017. http://bit.ly/2kphWY3

Chapter 4

Busari, Stephanie. "How Fake News Does Real Harm." TED Talk, 2017. http://bit.ly/2Fr2WPW

Robb, Amanda. "Anatomy of a Fake News Scandal." *Rolling Stone* magazine, Nov. 16, 2017. http://rol.st/2zTIIwa

Khan, Ali. "Fake Cockroach Lies on Snapchat Force Chadwell Heath Takeaway Boss to Put Business on Market." Barking and Dagenham Post, May 24, 2017. http://bit.ly/2FlWKsh

Grant, Joyce. "Discussing Challenging News Stories with Kids." Teaching Kids News. http://bit.ly/29J7lgu/

January, Beth. "How to Detect Fake News With These Tools and Techniques." Mediashift, Sept. 7, 2017. http://bit.ly/2eNTtde

Kasparov, Garry. Twitter. http://bit.ly/2Fm6XEZ

Learning More

Books

O'Donnell, Liam, and Mike Deas. *Media Meltdown: A Graphic Guide Adventure.*
Orca Book Publishers. 2009.

Donovan, Sandy, *Media, From News Coverage to Political Advertising,*
Lerner Publishing, 2016.

Paiser, Barb. *Choosing News: What Gets Reported and Why.*
Capstone Publishing, 2012.

Various authors, Asking Questions About Media series,
Cherry Lake Publishing, Ann Arbor, Michigan, 2015. Titles include Video Games,
What's on Television, How Movies Get Made, Body Image in Advertising.

Websites

https://ed.ted.com/lessons/how-false-news-can-spread-noah-tavlin#watch
https://ed.ted.com/on/fLQF70t0
These two short videos, How False News Can Spread, and Fact Or Opinion, are part of
the TED-Ed collection of educational videos for youth.

www.mediasmarts.ca/media-literacy-101
www.mediasmarts.ca/sites/mediasmarts/files/guides/media_toolkit_youth_2014.pdf
Media Literacy 101, features six one-minute videos designed to teach you about
different aspects of the media. The second link takes you to an excellent booklet titled
Making Your Voice Heard: A Media Toolkit for Youth. .

http://guides.libraries.psu.edu/c.php?g=620262&tp=4319238
The library at Penn State University created this webpage, titled Fake News. It presents
a quick overview of the subject through text, video, and links to other resources.

www.bbc.co.uk/education/subjects/zqyqh39
This link focuses on the craft of the reporter.

Glossary

Arab Spring A series of protests and uprisings in Arab countries of the Middle East beginning in 2010. The protesters were fighting for better government and more freedom to vote (democracy)

attributed Regarded as belonging or having come from a specific person or thing

beat A particular area of interest covered by a journalist; for example, the business beat

bias Preferences and opinions in favor of one thing more than another

child trafficking The illegal movement of children under 18, usually to sell them or exploit them, harm them, or use them for labor

citizen journalists People who report on events, often as they happen and post the information on the Internet. They are usually not trained journalists. Sometimes they report on events for recognized news providers

click bait A catchy headline, photo, or bit of content on social media such as Facebook or Instagram, or on websites that encourages Internet users to click on a link to read on; the link can lead to sites with articles and sensational news

compelling Something that commands attention because it is interesting or important

consequence The result of something, or the effect of an action

conspiracy theory An idea or belief that an event has been caused because of secret plots that are unknown to the general public

credible Something that is convincing and can be believed based on facts that can be tested or verified

democracy A form of government where citizens freely vote for representatives to serve them in government

digital world The world connected through digital devices and technology such as cell phones, tablets, computers, and the Internet

dishonorable Something someone does to bring shame or disgrace upon themselves

diverse A number of different options

editor A person at a newspaper who chooses stories to be featured in the newspaper and ensures stories have no factual or spelling/grammar errors

ethics Rules and principles on how to live your life

explicit Something that is clearly stated or expressed

gatekeeper Someone who controls the flow of information and prevents things from passing through

generalist (reporter) A journalist who is expected to cover stories in a variety of subject areas

Holocaust The systematic mass murder of six million European Jews by the Nazi regime in Europe during World War II

legitimate Something that is seen as acceptable or of a certain standard

lingo Specialized wording or terminology

mainstream Ideas and attitudes that are considered normal or dominant

manipulate To control or influence people, usually without their knowledge, to make them think or behave in a particular way

mass communication The delivery of information to a large and varied group of people

mechanism A system or process to make something happen

misinformation False or inaccurate information

moveable type Individual letters of the alphabet that are carved into pieces of hard material, usually metal; the letters are arranged into words, inked, and pressed onto paper to make a document

multi-sensory Relating to several senses, often at the same time, such as sight, hearing, and touch

Glossary

Nazi regime The rule of the Nazi political party, headed by Adolph Hitler, in Germany from 1933 until 1945.

news hook A piece of information used to grab the attention of a newspaper reader, TV viewer or radio listener; a tidbit that makes people pay attention to a story

newsworthy An event, story, or other piece of information that's interesting enough to be included in a newspaper or other news report

perspective point of view; an attitude toward a person, issue, or event; a way of looking at something

plagiarized taking someone else's work without permission and presenting it as your own

point of view the perspective or way of looking at things held by a person, or organization such as a politician, government, or media

policies rule, principal, or guideline that governments follow when making decisions

processes a series of actions directed toward an end

profit-making something that earns money

reputable Highly respected, well regarded, or having a good reputation for doing something well

slant The point of view of something that is seen or presented

source A person who gives a journalist information

Spanish American War A war between the United States and Spain in 1898, fought in the Caribbean and the Pacific, mainly over Cuban independence.

supermarket tabloid a newspaper focusing on celebrity news and gossip that is sold at a grocery store checkout counter; usually features attention-grabbing headlines and photos, and sometimes mean-spirited or false information

tone The attitude or perspective of a written or spoken piece

trending A topic that gets a lot of posts on social media within a short period of time

unsubstantiated something that cannot be proven

verified something that has been confirmed as accurate or acceptable evidence

worldview the way someone understands the world and how they believe it should work

World War II A major war from 1939-1945 between the axis powers of Germany, Italy and Japan, and the Allies, Britain, the Soviet Union, Canada, France, Australia, New Zealand, and others.

Index

About the Author

Diane Dakers spent 25 years as a newspaper, television, and radio journalist, before she began writing books. She teaches university-level communications and has written three fiction and 22 nonfiction books for young people, on topics as varied as financial literacy, Magic Johnson, and "green" transportation